# GREAT WARRIORS

ANN WEIL

**Chicago, Illinois**

© 2007 Raintree
Published by Raintree,
A division of Reed Elsevier, Inc.
Chicago, Illinois

Customer Service   888–454–2279

Visit our website at www.raintreelibrary.com

Printed in China by WKT

11 10 09 08 07
10 9 8 7 6 5 4 3 2 1

**Library of Congress
Cataloging-in-Publication Data**
Weil, Ann.
  Great warriors / Ann Weil.
    p. cm. -- (Atomic)
  Includes bibliographical references and index.
  ISBN 1-4109-2525-0 (library binding-hardcover)
-- ISBN 1-4109-2530-7 (pbk.)
 1.  Military biography--Juvenile literature.  I. Title.
II. Series: Atomic (Chicago, Ill.)
  U51.W44 2006
  355.0092'2--dc22

  2006002962

13 digit ISBNs:
978-1-4109-2525-1 (hardcover)
978-1-4109-2530-5 (paperback)

**Acknowledgments**
The author and publishers are grateful to the
following for permission to reproduce copyright
material: Alamy, pp. **6** (Rob Bartee), **13**
(Visual&Written/SL/D Larsen-African Pictures);
Corbis pp. **9 main** (Ben Wittick), **21** (Bettmann/
Philip Gendreau), **18** (Charles & Josette Lenars), **10**
(Edward S Curtis), **12** (Gallo Images/Roger De La
Harpe), **14** (Jim Zuckerman), **22** (Peter Guttman),
**8 inset** (Reuters/Sukree Sukplang), **29** (Zefa/Roy
McMahon); Dreamworks p. **26** (Universal/The Kobal
Collection/Buitendijk, JAAP); Getty Images p. **17
inset** (Lawrence Lucier); Rex Features pp. **5** (J
Goncalvez), **25** (The Travel Library); Warner Bros
courtesy of The Kobal Collection p. **17 main**.

Cover photograph of a Maasai warrior reproduced
with permission of Corbis (The Cover Story).

The publishers would like to thank Diana Bentley,
Nancy Harris, and Dee Reid for their assistance in
the preparation of this book.

Every effort has been made to contact copyright
holders of any material reproduced in this book.
Any omissions will be rectified in subsequent
printings if notice is given to the publishers.

**Disclaimer**

# Contents

Some words are printed in bold, **like this**. You can find out what they mean in the glossary. You can also look in the box at the bottom of the page where the word first appears.

# GREAT WARRIORS

Xingu warriors covered in war paint show their weapons in a war dance. Two Japanese **samurai**, their swords flashing, fight to the death. Gladiators face off in an ancient Roman **arena**.

## Warriors around the world

Throughout history there have been warriors all around the world: in Africa, Asia, Europe, Australasia, and the Americas. In some places young men could not marry until after they became warriors. For them becoming a warrior was the same as becoming a man.

### Fierce fact

Today, both men and women fight in wars. In the past, warriors were almost always men.

| | |
|---|---|
| arena | large, open area for holding entertainment and sports events |
| gladiator | person in ancient Rome who fought other gladiators, sometimes to the death |

Some tribes, such as this one from the Xingu nation in Brazil, still keep their warrior traditions alive today.

**samurai**    name for Japanese warriors from 1185 to 1868

United States

Native American warriors, such as this member of the Sioux tribe, believed that the colorful designs of their war paint protected them.

# SITTING BULL

Sitting Bull (about 1831–1890) is one of the most famous Native American warriors in history.

## The Battle of Little Bighorn

In the late 1800s, the U.S. Army was forcing Native Americans off their land and onto **reservations**. Sitting Bull refused to go. "No man controls our footsteps," he said.

In the summer of 1876, Sitting Bull led thousands of warriors against the U.S. Army at the Battle of Little Bighorn, in Montana. It was a tremendous victory for the Native Americans and a disaster for the U.S. Army.

With only a few hundred soldiers, the U.S. Army was vastly outnumbered, and almost all of them died on the battlefield.

reservation — area of land set aside by the U.S. government for Native Americans

# GERONIMO

Geronimo (1829–1909) was an Apache warrior. However, in his early adult life, he was a doctor and a family man.

## A legend is born

In 1858 Mexican soldiers murdered Geronimo's mother, wife, and their three children. Geronimo was enraged and he wanted **revenge**. He fought battles against ever-increasing numbers of Mexican and U.S. soldiers. He was renowned for his bravery and his ability to escape from imprisonment.

## Fierce fact

Why do people yell "Geronimo!" when they parachute? In 1940 a group of U.S. soldiers was nervous about a new parachute jump they had to do. To relax, they went to a movie about Geronimo and his brave fight. Later, as one of the men jumped out of the plane, he yelled "Geronimo!" to show he was not afraid.

Geronimo led his warriors in many daring raids. He was finally captured and put in prison in 1886.

| | |
|---|---|
| **Apache** | large group (tribe) of Native Americans who used to live in the southwestern United States and northern Mexico |
| **revenge** | to get even |

This Piegan chief wears weasel tails to match his name, Chief Weasel Tail. He carries a tomahawk.

tomahawk

# NATIVE AMERICAN WEAPONS

Native Americans used bows and arrows for hunting and warfare. Warriors also used clubs and hatchets called tomahawks. Some warriors used guns, which they acquired through trade with European settlers.

## Power of the enemy

Warriors used knives to **scalp** their enemies. A soldier explained: "As soon as the man has fallen, they run to him, put their knee between his shoulders, take a lock of hair in one hand, and with their knife in the other give a blow separating the skin from the head, and tearing off a piece." The warriors believed that the scalp would give them the powers of their enemy.

### Fierce fact

Warriors buried a tomahawk in the ground when they made peace with enemies. This is where the expression "burying the hatchet," meaning making peace, comes from.

scalp — to cut off the skin that covers the top of someone's head

# DAY OF THE ZULU

On January 22, 1879, the British army invaded Zululand in southeast Africa, hoping to gain control over the Zulu people and their land.

## Surprise defeat

The British were confident of an easy victory, believing themselves better armed and with superior skills. But the Zulu army was huge. More than 20,000 Zulu warriors attacked the 1,300 British soldiers and their African **allies**. Zulu warriors used spears and clubs, and the British guns were of little use in **hand-to-hand combat**.

The Zulu army won the battle in three hours. They killed all but 55 of the British soldiers.

### Fierce fact

The Zulu stabbing spear is called an *iklwa*. The name comes from the sound the spear makes when pulled out of a body.

Zululand

These modern-day Zulu warriors wear traditional dress.

ally       person or group that joins with another group to fight a war

hand-to-hand combat       fighting at close range

East Africa

The Maasai are nomadic people who live in East Africa.

| | |
|---|---|
| nomadic | describes people who do not settle in one area, but rather move from place to place, often in search of food |
| rite of passage | event or ceremony that marks the end of one stage of life and the beginning of another |

# MAASAI LION HUNTERS

**Vultures** fly in circles above a lion and its most recent kill. Maasai warriors watch the sky and follow these birds to where the lion is eating.

## Becoming a warrior, becoming a man

The warriors force the lion away from its kill. They know this will anger the lion—they are looking for a good fight. The lion faces one of the warriors, roars, and attacks!

Lion hunting used to be a **rite of passage** for young Maasai men. It demonstrated that they had become good hunters and were ready to get married. However, it is no longer legal to hunt lions.

### Fierce fact

Lion hunting was very dangerous. Lions are intelligent, deadly animals. Maasai warriors have died fighting lions.

vulture    large bird that feeds mostly on the meat of dead animals

# SAMURAI

For hundreds of years, there were warriors in Japan called **samurai**. They rode horses, wore armor, and used many different weapons. Their most famous weapon was a long, sharp sword.

## Death over dishonor

Samurai were brave and loyal. A true samurai would rather die fighting than **surrender**. A samurai, defeated or disgraced in any way, would kill himself by cutting open his own stomach. This tradition is called *seppuku* or *hara-kiri*. It was a very painful way to die. Sometimes another samurai would cut off the man's head to prevent him from suffering too long.

### Fierce fact

Samurai swords were deadly sharp. They could slice a person's head off with one blow.

**surrender**   give up

Japan

Samurai helmets often had scary-looking masks to frighten the enemy. The mask also protected the samurai's face.

## Fierce fact

Asmat warriors believed the spirits of their ancestors inhabited war shields. They thought the designs on the shields would shock enemies into dropping their weapons. Then, the Asmat could tie them up and cut off their heads.

# ASMAT: NEW GUINEA HEADHUNTERS

## Until the 1900s, headhunters in New Guinea had little contact with outsiders and lived like people from the Stone Age.

### Early contact with Europeans

In 1770 a British ship went to New Guinea. Some sailors went ashore, but they were so terrified of the fierce Asmat warriors that they quickly retreated to their ship.

Asmat headhunters used bone daggers (short knives). Some daggers were made from the leg bone of a large bird called a cassowary. Others were made from human bones.

New Guinea

| ancestor | grandparent or other relative who lived a long time ago |
| --- | --- |
| headhunter | warrior who seeks to cut off the head of an enemy and keep it as a trophy |
| Stone Age | period that happened thousands of years ago, when people first made tools and weapons from stone |

# Shrunken Heads of the Shuar

It took Shuar warriors of Ecuador about a week to shrink the head of an enemy.

## How to shrink a head

First, they peeled off the skin and hair and sewed the eyes shut. Wooden pegs kept the lips closed together while the head was boiled for an hour or two. This shrunk the head to one-third its original size. Then, the skin was turned inside out and any leftover flesh was scraped off. They dropped hot stones inside the head to shrink it some more. When the head got too small for stones, they used hot sand instead.

### Fierce fact

The Shuar believed that a head gave the taker special powers.

Ecuador

The Shuar took great care so
the shrunken heads would still
resemble their enemies.

These modern-day Dayak warriors still show off their skills with blowing tubes to visitors.

Borneo

# HEADHUNTERS OF BORNEO

After cutting off the heads of their enemies, the Dayak warriors of Borneo carefully **extracted** the brains through the nostrils. Then, they put the heads in a net hung over a fire to dry.

## Strong magic

The Dayak believed that dried skulls had strong magic. The magic could protect them from their enemies. It could also make rain and help rice grow.

## Weapons

Dayak headhunters used long metal swords. They decorated the sword handles with clumps of human hair from their victims. They also shot poisoned arrows at their enemies through a blowing tube.

**extract**     remove or take out

# MAORI WARRIORS

Long ago the Maori of New Zealand did not welcome visitors. In 1642 some Dutch sailors were approaching New Zealand in their ships. Before the Dutch had even set foot on land, Maori warriors attacked and killed them from war canoes out at sea.

## Tattoos

Maori warriors had tattoos on their face and body. Getting a tattoo was painful and bloody. They used a tool made from bone to cut the skin. Then, they dropped burnt caterpillars or gum from trees into the cuts to make the tattoo.

### Fierce fact

Facial tattoos healed slowly. During that time, warriors were fed liquid food through a funnel. This kept food away from the swollen skin. It also prevented the wound from being opened by chewing.

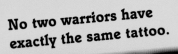

New Zealand

**funnel**    cone-shaped tube used to pour
liquids through a small opening

Thousands of people gathered to watch these skilled warriors.

## Fierce fact

Gladiators had different roles, which required different weapons and armor. The "fish man" wore a helmet with what looked like a fish's fin on the top. He often fought against a gladiator called the "net man."

# GLADIATORS

## In ancient Rome, a victorious gladiator stands over his defeated opponent, waiting for the crowd's decision.

### Live or die

The **spectators** would decide if the loser had put up a good fight. If he had, he would probably be allowed to live so that he could fight again. If he had not, they would signal for the winner to kill him.

### From slave to gladiator

Most gladiators were slaves. They learned how to fight at gladiator schools. There they were fed well, so they would become strong.

Gladiator games were very popular in ancient Rome.

| spectator | person watching something, such as a sporting event |

# The End of the Age of Warriors?

**Gladiator** games were **banned** shortly before the fall of the Roman Empire about C.E. 476. **Headhunting** has been outlawed. The Maori welcome guests to their homeland in New Zealand.

## Modern warriors?

Today, young people prove themselves in different ways, such as through sports and academic achievement, rather than violence.

All over the world, people practice **martial arts** for exercise and self-defense. Some boys and girls start to study martial arts, such as judo and karate, at a very young age. They learn some of the same fighting styles used by ancient warriors. However, these modern-day warriors do not use their skills for fighting. They show them in sports competitions, including the Olympics.

Martial arts training often goes beyond physical activity, and also includes mental and emotional development.

ban — to prevent something by making it against the law

martial art — fighting sport or technique of self-defense, such as karate or judo

# Glossary

**ally** person or group that joins with another group to fight a war

**ancestor** grandparent or other relative who lived a long time ago

**Apache** large group (tribe) of Native Americans who used to live in the southwestern United States and northern Mexico

**arena** large, open area for holding entertainment and sports events

**ban** to prevent something by making it against the law

**extract** remove or take out

**funnel** cone-shaped tube used to pour liquids through a small opening

**gladiator** person in ancient Rome who fought other gladiators, sometimes to the death

**hand-to-hand combat** fighting at close range

**headhunter** warrior who seeks to cut off the head of an enemy and keep it as a trophy

**martial art** fighting sport or technique of self-defense, such as karate or judo

**nomadic** describes people who do not settle in one area, but rather move from place to place, often in search of food

**reservation** area of land set aside by the U.S. government for Native Americans

**revenge** to get even

**rite of passage** event or ceremony that marks the end of one stage of life and the beginning of another

**samurai** name for Japanese warriors from 1185 to 1868

**scalp** to cut off the skin that covers the top of someone's head

**spectator** person watching something, such as a sporting event

**Stone Age** period that happened thousands of years ago, when people first made tools and weapons from stone

**surrender** give up

**vulture** large bird that feeds mostly on the meat of dead animals

# Want to know more?

## Books

✴ Hall, Lynn Bedford. *Shaka, Warrior King of the Zulu*. Cape Town, South Africa: Struik, 2005.

✴ Macdonald, Fiona. *How to Be a Samurai Warrior*. Washington, D.C.: National Geographic, 2005.

✴ Marrin, Albert. *Sitting Bull and His World*. New York: Dutton, 2000.

✴ Stanley, George E. *Geronimo: Young Warrior*. New York: Aladdin, 2001.

## Websites

✴ www.pbs.org/wnet/warriorchallenge/
gladiators/index.html
This page is all about gladiators.
It also has interactive games.

✴ www.pbs.org/wnet/warriorchallenge/
knights/index.html
This is a page about knights,
complete with interactive games.

**If you liked this Atomic book, why don't you try these...?**

# Index